Holt Spanish 2

Activities for Communication

HOLT, RINEHART AND WINSTON
A Harcourt Education Company

Orlando • **Austin** • New York • San Diego • Toronto • London

Copyright © by Holt, Rinehart and Winston

All rights reserved. No part of this publication may be reproduced or transmitted in any form or by any means, electronic or mechanical, including photocopy, recording, or any information storage and retrieval system, without permission in writing from the publisher.

Teachers using ¡EXPRÉSATE! may photocopy complete pages in sufficient quantities for classroom use only and not for resale.

HOLT, ¡EXPRÉSATE!, and the **"Owl Design"** are trademarks licensed to Holt, Rinehart and Winston, registered in the United States of America and/or other jurisdictions.

Printed in the United States of America

> If you have received these materials as examination copies free of charge, Holt, Rinehart and Winston retains title to the materials and they may not be resold. Resale of examination copies is strictly prohibited.

> Possession of this publication in print format does not entitle users to convert this publication, or any portion of it, into electronic format.

ISBN 0-03-074412-1

10 11 12 13 14   1409   13 12 11 10 09

Table of Contents

To the Teacher iv

COMMUNICATIVE ACTIVITIES

Capítulo 1
Vocabulario 1/Gramática 1 1A, 1B . . 1
Vocabulario 2/Gramática 2 2A, 2B . . 3

Capítulo 2
Vocabulario 1/Gramática 1 1A, 1B . . 5
Vocabulario 2/Gramática 2 2A, 2B . . 7

Capítulo 3
Vocabulario 1/Gramática 1 1A, 1B . . 9
Vocabulario 2/Gramática 2 2A, 2B . . 11

Capítulo 4
Vocabulario 1/Gramática 1 1A, 1B . . 13
Vocabulario 2/Gramática 2 2A, 2B . . 15

Capítulo 5
Vocabulario 1/Gramática 1 1A, 1B . . 17
Vocabulario 2/Gramática 2 2A, 2B . . 19

Capítulo 6
Vocabulario 1/Gramática 1 1A, 1B . . 21
Vocabulario 2/Gramática 2 2A, 2B . . 23

Capítulo 7
Vocabulario 1/Gramática 1 1A, 1B . . 25
Vocabulario 2/Gramática 2 2A, 2B . . 27

Capítulo 8
Vocabulario 1/Gramática 1 1A, 1B . . 29
Vocabulario 2/Gramática 2 2A, 2B . . 31

Capítulo 9
Vocabulario 1/Gramática 1 1A, 1B . . 33
Vocabulario 2/Gramática 2 2A, 2B . . 35

Capítulo 10
Vocabulario 1/Gramática 1 1A, 1B . . 37
Vocabulario 2/Gramática 2 2A, 2B . . 39

PICTURE SEQUENCES
Capítulo 1 43
Capítulo 2 44
Capítulo 3 45
Capítulo 4 46
Capítulo 5 47
Capítulo 6 48
Capítulo 7 49
Capítulo 8 50
Capítulo 9 51
Capítulo 10 52

INTERPERSONAL COMMUNICATION

Capítulo 1
Interviews 55
Role-Plays 56

Capítulo 2
Interviews 57
Role-Plays 58

Capítulo 3
Interviews 59
Role-Plays 60

Capítulo 4
Interviews 61
Role-Plays 62

Capítulo 5
Interviews 63
Role-Plays 64

Capítulo 6
Interviews 65
Role-Plays 66

Capítulo 7
Interviews 67
Role-Plays 68

Capítulo 8
Interviews 69
Role-Plays 70

Capítulo 9
Interviews 71
Role-Plays 72

Capítulo 10
Interviews 73
Role-Plays 74

To the Teacher

Oral communication is the most challenging language skill to develop and test. The *¡Exprésate! Activities for Communication* book helps students develop their speaking skills and gives them opportunities to communicate in many different situations. The Communicative Activities and Interpersonal Communication Cards provide a variety of information-gap activities, role-plays, and interviews to assist students with the progression from closed-ended practice to more creative, open-ended use of Spanish. The Picture Sequences provide image-based scenarios that allow students to creatively incorporate learned vocabulary, grammar, and functions from each chapter while working in pairs or groups. With the focus on conversation and real-life context, the activities in this book will help your students achieve the goal of genuine interaction, as well as prepare them for the oral exam following each chapter test and the oral assessment items in the Alternative Assessment section of the *Assessment Program*.

Each chapter of *Activities for Communication* provides:

Communicative Activities In each of the ten chapters, two communicative, pair-work activities encourage students to use Spanish in realistic conversation, in settings where they must seek and share information. The activities provide cooperative language practice and encourage students to take risks with language in a relaxed, uninhibiting, and enjoyable setting. The activities correspond to each vocabulary and grammar section and encourage use of functions, vocabulary, and grammar presented in that chapter section. Each activity may be used upon completion of each grammar and vocabulary section to promote oral proficiency and to prepare students for oral assessment; this could be for the oral exam following each chapter, and/or the oral performance and portfolio activities in the Alternative Assessment section of the *Assessment Program*. The activities may also be recorded on audio or video tape for inclusion in students' portfolios, or may be used as an informal review of each section to provide additional oral practice.

Picture Sequences Each of the ten chapters contains one picture sequence activity that provides a chapter-oriented story for students to work on in pairs or groups. The picture sequences are designed to guide students, within the context of a chapter-themed story, to creatively integrate and use chapter vocabulary, grammar, and functions. Each picture sequence may be used upon completion of the chapter as a global performance assessment, or may be used to prepare students for the picture sequence assessment activity in the Alternative Assessment portion of the *Assessment Program*. The stories may also be recorded on audio or video tape for inclusion in students' portfolios. Rubrics for grading the picture stories are available in the Alternative Assessment portion of the *Assessment Program*.

Interpersonal Communication Cards Each of the ten chapters contains three interviews and three situations for role-playing, one for each grammar and vocabulary section and one global review for the entire chapter, in blackline master form. These cards are designed to stimulate conversation and to prepare students for the oral exam following the chapter test, as well as for the oral performance and portfolio activities in the Alternative Assessment section of the *Assessment Program*. (Rubrics for grading these activities are available in the Alternative Assessment portion of the *Assessment Program*.) The interviews or role-playing may be used as pair work with the entire class, as activities to begin the class period, as oral performance assessments upon completion of each chapter section, and as a review of each chapter. They may also be used to encourage oral practice at any point during the study of each section. These conversations may be recorded as audio or video additions to students' portfolios. Because the cards may be recycled throughout the scholastic year as review of chapters already completed, students will be rewarded as they realize they are meeting goals and improving their communicative abilities. To avoid having to copy the cards repeatedly, consider mounting them on cardboard and laminating them. They may be filed for use during the year as well as for future classes.

Nombre _____ Clase _____ Fecha _____

Familiares y amigos

COMMUNICATIVE ACTIVITY 1A

SITUATION You and your partner are on the planning committee of your neighborhood's new recreational center. In order to build a center that everyone will like and use, you are conducting a survey of all the neighborhood families.

TASK 1 Answer your partner's questions about your imaginary family.

MODELO A — ¿Cómo es tu hermana María?
B — Mi hermana María es muy activa.
A — ¿Qué le gusta hacer los fines de semana?
B — A María le gusta correr.

La familia Robles	Es...	Le gusta...
Mi hermana María	muy activo(a)	correr
Mi hermano Sebastián	gracioso(a)	contar chistes
Yo	tímido(a)	leer novelas de misterio
Mi mamá Luisa	trabajador(a)	escribir cartas
Mi papá Roberto	intelectual	jugar al ajedrez

TASK 2 Now, switch roles. Your partner represents the García family. Ask your partner what his or her imaginary family is like and what they like to do on weekends. Take notes using complete sentences.

La familia García	¿Cómo es?	¿Qué le gusta?
Tú		
Tu hermana Lupe		
Tu mamá		
Tu papá		

Holt Spanish 2   Activities for Communication

Nombre _____ Clase _____ Fecha _____

Familiares y amigos

CAPÍTULO 1

COMMUNICATIVE ACTIVITY 1B

SITUATION You and your partner are on the planning committee of your neighborhood's new recreational center. In order to build a center that everyone will like and use, you are conducting a survey of all the neighborhood families.

TASK 1 Your partner represents the Robles family. Ask your partner what his or her imaginary family is like and what they like to do on weekends. Take notes using complete sentences.

MODELO A — ¿Cómo es tu hermana María?
B — Mi hermana María es muy activa.
A — ¿Qué le gusta hacer los fines de semana?
B — A María le gusta correr.

La familia Robles	¿Cómo es?	¿Qué le gusta?
Tu hermana María	Es muy activa.	Le gusta correr.
Tu hermano Sebastián		
Tú		
Tu mamá		
Tu papá		

TASK 2 Now, switch roles. Answer your partner's questions about your imaginary family.

La familia García	Es...	Le gusta...
Yo	extrovertido(a)	mantenerme en forma
Mi hermana Lupe	simpático(a)	jugar al volibol
Mi mamá	serio(a)	ver televisión
Mi papá	activo(a)	montar en bicicleta

Holt Spanish 2   Activities for Communication

Nombre _____ Clase _____ Fecha _____

Familiares y amigos

CAPÍTULO

COMMUNICATIVE ACTIVITY 2A

SITUATION Your family is throwing three big parties this week and you are running around the house frantically! Luckily, your best friend has stopped by to help out.

TASK 1 Start by telling your partner when you are going to celebrate each event. When your partner asks if he or she can help, tell him or her to do the things listed for each party.

MODELO A — Esta noche vamos a celebrar una fiesta sorpresa.
　　　　　　B — ¿Puedo ayudarte?
　　　　　　A — Sí, pasa la aspiradora.
　　　　　　B — ¿Algo más?
　　　　　　A — Sí, pon la mesa.

¿Cuándo?/Fiesta	Cosas que hacer
Esta noche / una fiesta sorpresa	pasar la aspiradora poner la mesa
Mañana / el día de la independencia	decorar el patio cortar el césped
Pasado mañana / el cumpleaños de Sara	comprar la piñata preparar el pastel

TASK 2 Now, switch roles. Listen to your partner tell you when his or her family is going to celebrate each event. Then ask him or her how you can help out, using the expressions in the example above. Take notes on what needs to be done so that you don't forget.

| Cosas que hacer | ¿Cuándo?/Fiesta |||
	Esta noche/ la Nochevieja	Mañana/ el aniversario de tus padres	Pasado mañana/ el cumpleaños de Francisco
llamar a los invitados			
ayudar a tu madre			
preparar la cena			
ir de compras al mercado			
comprar el regalo			
limpiar la cocina			

Holt Spanish 2　　　　　　　　　　　　　　　　　　　　　　　Activities for Communication

Nombre _____ Clase _____ Fecha _____

Familiares y amigos

CAPÍTULO

COMMUNICATIVE ACTIVITY 2B

SITUATION Your best friend's family is throwing three big parties this week. He or she is responsible for getting everything done! Being the good friend that you are, you have come over to your partner's house to help out.

TASK 1 Listen to your partner tell you when his or her family is going to celebrate each event. Then ask him or her how you can help out, using the expressions in the example. Take notes on what needs to be done so that you don't forget.

MODELO A — Esta noche vamos a celebrar una fiesta sorpresa.
B — ¿Puedo ayudarte?
A — Sí, pasa la aspiradora.
B — ¿Algo más?
A — Sí, pon la mesa.

Cosas que hacer	¿Cuándo?/Fiesta		
	Esta noche/ una fiesta sorpresa	Mañana/ el día de la independencia	Pasado mañana/ el cumpleaños de Sara
decorar el patio			
pasar la aspiradora	✓		
poner la mesa	✓		
cortar el césped			
comprar la piñata			
preparar el pastel			

TASK 2 Now, switch roles. Tell your partner when you are going to celebrate each event. When your partner asks if he or she can help, tell him or her to do the things listed for each party.

¿Cuándo?/Fiesta	Cosas que hacer
Esta noche / la Nochevieja	ayudar a mi madre ir de compras al mercado
Mañana / el aniversario de mis padres	preparar la cena limpiar la cocina
Pasado mañana / el cumpleaños de Francisco	llamar a los invitados comprar el regalo

Holt Spanish 2

Activities for Communication

Nombre _____ Clase _____ Fecha _____

En el vecindario

CAPÍTULO 2

COMMUNICATIVE ACTIVITY 1A

SITUATION You are writing a report on what people in different professions do. You have gone to a local town to interview people about their jobs.

TASK 1 Ask your partner what each of the following people are doing. Then, guess their profession.

MODELO A — ¿Qué está haciendo la señora Tito?
B — Le presta dinero al señor Robles. ¿Sabes a qué se dedica?
A — Sí, es banquera.

Trabajador(a)	¿Qué está haciendo?	Es...
la señora Tito	Le presta dinero al señor Robles.	banquera.
la señora Ricardo		
el señor Flores		
el señor Soto		
la señora Rivera		
el señor Delgado		

cartero/
mujer cartero
peluquero(a)
abogado(a)
banquero(a)
cocinero(a)
dentista

TASK 2 Now, switch roles. Answer your partner's questions about what the following people do. Then, ask if he or she can guess what each person's profession is based on what you said.

Trabajador(a)	¿Qué está haciendo?	Profesión
la señora Tito	prestar dinero al señor Robles	banquera
la señora Moreno	cuidar a los enfermos	médica
la señora Torres	escribir artículos	periodista
el señor Castro	trabajar en un taller y arreglar carros	mecánico
la señora Méndez	diseñar páginas Web	programadora
el señor Vega	apagar incendios	bombero

Holt Spanish 2   Activities for Communication

Nombre _____ Clase _____ Fecha _____

En el vecindario

COMMUNICATIVE ACTIVITY 1B

SITUATION Your partner is writing a report on what people in different professions do and wants to interview workers in your town.

TASK 1 Answer your partner's questions about what the following people are doing. Then, ask if he or she can guess what each person's profession is based on what you said.

MODELO A — ¿Qué está haciendo la señora Tito?
B — Le presta dinero al señor Robles. ¿Sabes a qué se dedica?
A — Sí, es banquera.

Trabajador(a)	¿Qué está haciendo?	Profesión
la señora Tito	prestar dinero al señor Robles	banquera
la señora Ricardo	cortar el pelo al señor Fortuna	peluquera
el señor Flores	preparar la comida a la señora Blanca	cocinero
el señor Soto	traer correo a la señora Iglesias	cartero
la señora Rivera	cuidar los dientes al señor Escamilla	dentista
el señor Delgado	dar consejos a unos clientes	abogado

TASK 2 Now, switch roles. Ask your partner what each of the following people does. Then guess their profession.

Trabajador(a)	¿Qué está haciendo?	Es...
la señora Tito	*Le presta dinero al señor Robles.*	*banquera.*
la señora Moreno		
la señora Torres		
el señor Castro		
la señora Méndez		
el señor Vega		

programador(a)
banquero(a)
bombero(a)
periodista
mecánico(a)
médico(a)

Holt Spanish 2 — Activities for Communication

Nombre _____ Clase _____ Fecha _____

En el vecindario

COMMUNICATIVE ACTIVITY 2A

SITUATION Your parents have given you and your sibling (your partner) a list of chores and your sibling has decided that he or she doesn't want to do any of them.

TASK 1 Tell your sibling (your partner) that he or she has to do the following chores, using any of the expressions listed below. If your partner complains about a chore, tell him or her that your parents said he or she has to do it. Keep track of everything that he or she has already done.

MODELO A — Haz el favor de lavar los platos.
 B — Ya los lavé.
 A — ¡Ay, gracias! Ahora tienes que limpiar la bañera.
 B — ¡Estoy harto(a) de limpiar la bañera!
 A — Pues, mamá dice que tienes que limpiarla.

Cosas para hacer:	Ya lo hizo.
lavar los platos	*Ya los lavé.*
limpiar la bañera	
barrer el piso del baño	
poner la ropa en la lavadora	
colgar el cuadro nuevo	
darle de comer al gato	
organizar el estante	
sacudir los muebles	

Haz el favor de +
Hay que +
Debes +
Tienes que +

TASK 2 Now, switch roles. Listen to your partner's requests and demands. Tell your partner when you have already done one of the chores that he or she asks you to do. If you haven't done something, complain by using one of the expressions listed below. Keep track of everything that you still have to do.

Ya lo hice.	Todavía tengo que...
regar las plantas	
limpiar la estufa	
sacar la basura	
organizar la habitación	

¡Ay, qué pesado!
Estoy harto(a) de...
¡No es justo!
Ya lo hice mil veces.

Holt Spanish 2

Activities for Communication

Nombre _____ Clase _____ Fecha _____

En el vecindario

COMMUNICATIVE ACTIVITY 2B

SITUATION Your parents have given you and your sibling (your partner) a list of chores and you have decided that you don't want to do any of them.

TASK 1 Listen to your partner's requests and demands. Tell your partner when you have already done one of the chores that he or she asks you to do. If you haven't done something, complain by using one of the expressions listed below. Keep track of everything that you still have to do.

MODELO A — Haz el favor de lavar los platos.
B — Ya los lavé.
A — ¡Ay, gracias! Ahora tienes que limpiar la bañera.
B — Estoy harto(a) de limpiar la bañera!
A — Pues, mamá dice que tienes que limpiarla.

Ya lo hice.	Todavía tengo que...
lavar los platos	limpiar la bañera
barrer el piso	
colgar el cuadro nuevo	
organizar el estante	

¡Ay, qué pesado!
Estoy harto(a) de...
¡No es justo!
Ya lo hice mil veces.

TASK 2 Now, switch roles. Tell your sibling (your partner) that he or she has to do the following chores by using any of the expressions listed below. If your partner complains about a chore, tell him or her that your mom says he or she has to do it. Keep track of everything that he or she has already done.

Cosas para hacer:	Ya lo hizo.
regar las plantas	
sacudir los muebles	
limpiar la estufa	
poner los platos en el lavaplatos	
sacar la basura	
barrer el piso de la cocina	
organizar la habitación	
poner la ropa en la lavadora	

Haz el favor de +
Hay que +
Debes +
Tienes que +

Holt Spanish 2   Activities for Communication

Nombre _____ Clase _____ Fecha _____

Pueblos y ciudades

CAPÍTULO

COMMUNICATIVE ACTIVITY 1A

SITUATION You and your partner both had to run errands yesterday, but you didn't see each other. This surprises you because your town is so small.

TASK 1 Answer your partner's questions about where you went and what you did yesterday. Say at what time you went to each place so that your partner can take detailed notes.

MODELO B — ¿Adónde fuiste ayer?
A — A las nueve fui al mercado.
B — ¿Qué hiciste allí?
A — Compré muchas verduras.
B — Y después, ¿qué hiciste?
A — ...

¿Cuándo?	¿Adónde?	Lo que hice
9:00	ir al mercado	comprar muchas verduras
9:15	pasar por la pastelería	comprar un pastel de chocolate
9:45	tener que ir a la estación de tren	llevar a mis abuelos allí
10:30	ir a la peluquería	cortarme el pelo
12:20	llegar tarde al café Flores	almorzar con mi mamá
2:00	ir a la heladería	tomar un batido
5:00	ir a la plaza de Cristóbal Colón	dar una vuelta con mi perro

TASK 2 Now, ask your partner where he or she went and what he or she did yesterday. Keep asking him or her questions until you fill out the chart below.

¿Cuándo?	¿Adónde?	¿Qué hizo?

Holt Spanish 2

Activities for Communication

Nombre _____ Clase _____ Fecha _____

Pueblos y ciudades

CAPÍTULO 3

COMMUNICATIVE ACTIVITY 1B

SITUATION You and your partner both had to run errands yesterday, but you didn't see each other. This surprises you because your town is so small.

TASK 1 Ask your partner where he or she went and what he or she did yesterday. Keep asking him or her questions until you fill out the chart below.

MODELO B — ¿Adónde fuiste ayer?
A — A las nueve fui al mercado.
B — ¿Qué hiciste allí?
A — Compré muchas verduras.
B — Y después, ¿qué hiciste?
A — ...

¿Cuándo?	¿Adónde?	¿Qué hizo?
9:00	Fue al mercado.	Compró muchas verduras.

TASK 2 Now, answer your partner's questions about where you went and what you did yesterday. Say at what time you went to each place so that your partner can take detailed notes.

¿Cuándo?	¿Adónde?	Lo que hice
9:00	pasar por el banco	sacar dinero
9:15	ir a la librería	buscar unas revistas
10:00	ir a la estación de tren	recoger a mis primos
12:00	tener que volver a casa	almorzar con toda la familia
3:10	ir al cine	ver una película con mis primos
6:30	ir a la plaza de Cristóbal Colón	encontrarme con unos amigos

Holt Spanish 2   Activities for Communication

Nombre _____ Clase _____ Fecha _____

Pueblos y ciudades

CAPÍTULO

COMMUNICATIVE ACTIVITY 2A

SITUATION You work for a tourist office in the historic district of a big city. Your partner is a tourist who has come to your office to ask how to get to certain places.

TASK 1 Give your partner directions to the places he or she asks about.

MODELO B — Perdón, ¿cómo puedo llegar al Museo de Arte?
A — Salga de la oficina y doble a la izquierda. Siga derecho por cinco cuadras. Está enfrente del Parque Pista.
B — Muchas gracias. Y...

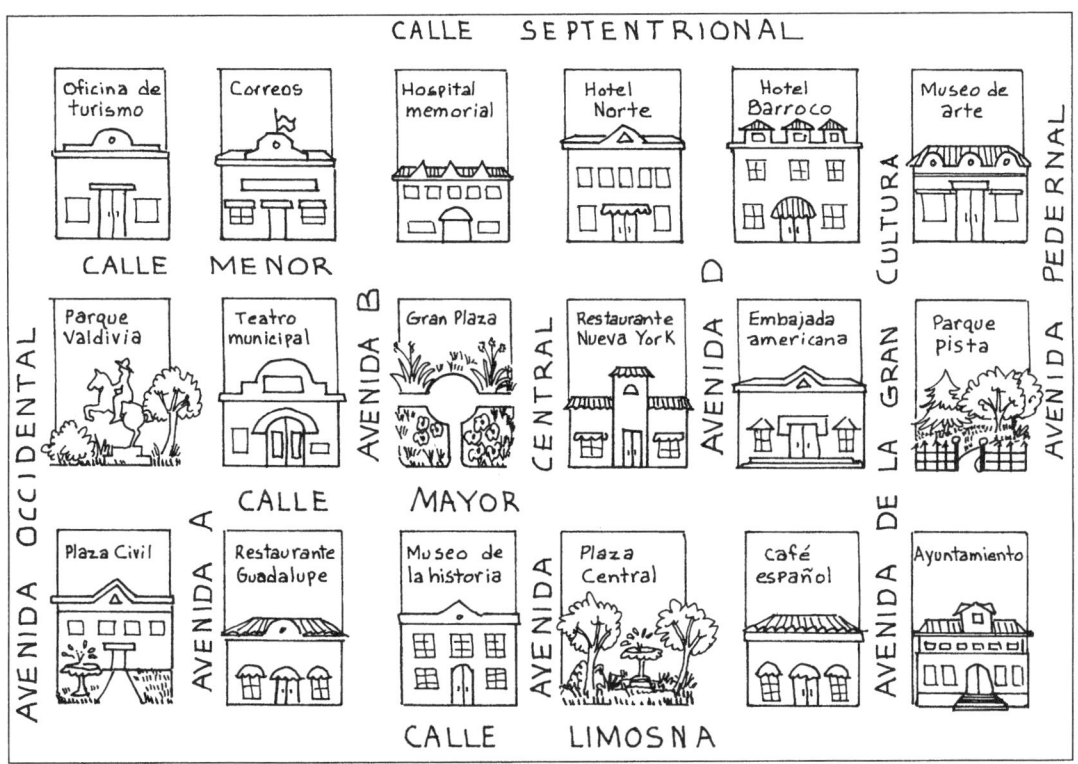

TASK 2 Now, switch roles. Using the same map, ask for directions from the **Oficina de turismo** to the **Embajada americana,** then to **Restaurante Guadalupe,** from there to the **Ayuntamiento,** and finally to the **Plaza Civil.** Trace your route on the map as you go.

Holt Spanish 2 — Activities for Communication
Copyright © by Holt, Rinehart and Winston. All rights reserved.

Nombre _____ Clase _____ Fecha _____

Pueblos y ciudades

CAPÍTULO 3

COMMUNICATIVE ACTIVITY 2B

SITUATION You are a tourist visiting the historic district of a big city and have stopped by the tourist office for directions to certain places. Your partner is an employee at the tourist office.

TASK 1 Ask for directions from the **Oficina de turismo** to the **Café español,** then to **Parque Valdivia,** from there to the **Museo de la historia,** and finally to the **Hotel Barroco.** Trace your route on the map as you go.

MODELO B — Perdón, ¿cómo puedo llegar al Museo de Arte?
 A — Salga de la oficina y doble a la izquierda. Siga derecho por cinco cuadras. Está enfrente del Parque Pista.
 B — Muchas gracias. Y...

TASK 2 Now, switch roles. You are the employee at the tourist office giving directions to the tourist. Using the same map, answer your partner's questions.

Holt Spanish 2
Activities for Communication
Copyright © by Holt, Rinehart and Winston All rights reserved

Nombre _____ Clase _____ Fecha _____

¡Mantente en forma!

CAPÍTULO 4

COMMUNICATIVE ACTIVITY 1A

SITUATION Last weekend both you and your partner had to compete against your friends in different sport events.

TASK 1 Answer your partner's questions about the competitions you and your friend participated in. When your partner asks how each event was, choose an adjective from the **Modelo.** To tell how you both reacted to winning or losing each event, refer to the chart below. Fortunately, you *won* all of the events.

MODELO A — ¿Qué tal estuvo la competencia de natación?
  B — Estuvo buenísima/increíble/fenomenal. ¡Gané!
  A — ¿Cómo te sentiste cuando ganaste?
  B — Me dio mucha alegría.
  A — Y tu amigo(a), ¿cómo se sintió cuando perdió?
  B — Se puso a gritar.

La competencia de...	A mí... / Yo...	(A) él / ella...
natación	darle mucha alegría	ponerse a gritar
gimnasia	ponerse muy contento(a)	darle tristeza
golf	ponerse a gritar de alegría	ponerse a llorar
oratoria	darle ganas de bailar	darle una rabia
patinaje sobre hielo	ponerse a llorar de alegría	ponerse callado(a)

TASK 2 Now, switch roles. Ask your partner how each of the following events turned out for your partner and his or her friend. Then, ask how they both felt after winning or losing each event. Take notes.

MODELO A — ¿Qué tal estuvo la competencia de natación?
  B — Estuvo fatal/horrible. ¡Perdí!
  A — ¿Cómo te sentiste cuando perdiste?
  B — Me puse a gritar.
  A — Y tu amigo(a), ¿cómo se sintió cuando ganó?
  B — Le dio mucha alegría.

La competencia de...	(A) él / ella...	(A) su amigo(a)...
natación	se puso a gritar	le dio mucha alegría
banda escolar		
esquí acuático		
lucha libre		
atletismo		

Holt Spanish 2 Activities for Communication

Nombre _____ Clase _____ Fecha _____

CAPÍTULO

¡Mantente en forma!

COMMUNICATIVE ACTIVITY 1B

SITUATION Last weekend both you and your partner had to compete against your friends in different sport events.

TASK 1 Ask your partner how each of the following events turned out for your partner and his or her friend. Then, ask how they both felt after winning or losing each event. Take notes.

MODELO A — ¿Qué tal estuvo la competencia de natación?
B — Estuvo buenísima/increíble/fenomenal. ¡Gané!
A — ¿Cómo te sentiste cuando ganaste?
B — Me dio mucha alegría.
A — Y tu amigo(a), ¿cómo se sintió cuando perdió?
B — Se puso a gritar.

La competencia de...	(A) él / ella...	(A) su amigo(a)...
natación	le dio mucha alegría	se puso a gritar
gimnasia		
golf		
oratoria		
patinaje sobre hielo		

TASK 2 Now, switch roles. Answer your partner's questions about the competitions you and your friend participated in. When your partner asks how each event was, choose an adjective from the **Modelo**. To tell how you both reacted to winning or losing each event, refer to the chart below. Unfortunately, you *lost* all of the events.

MODELO A — ¿Qué tal estuvo la competencia de natación?
B — Estuvo fatal/horrible. ¡Perdí!
A — ¿Cómo te sentiste cuando perdiste?
B — Me puse a gritar.
A — Y tu amigo(a), ¿cómo se sintió cuando ganó?
B — Le dio mucha alegría.

La competencia de...	A mí... / Yo...	(A) él / ella...
natación	ponerse a gritar	darle mucha alegría
banda escolar	ponerse triste	reírse
esquí acuático	darle vergüenza	ponerse a gritar y cantar
lucha libre	darle ganas de gritar	ponerse muy contento(a)
atletismo	ponerse a llorar	ponerse a llorar de alegría

Holt Spanish 2   Activities for Communication

Nombre _____ Clase _____ Fecha _____

¡Mantente en forma!

CAPÍTULO 4

COMMUNICATIVE ACTIVITY 2A

SITUATION You and your neighbor (your partner) have just gotten back from disastrous weekend trips. You both are in really bad physical shape.

TASK 1 Answer your partner's questions about what happened to you during the weekend. Listen to his or her advice for each of your ailments. Take notes.

MODELO   A — ¿Qué te pasó en el dedo?
B — Me corté.
A — ¡Ahora lo tienes infectado! Ponte ungüento y una curita.

¿Qué te pasó?	Consejos
cortarse el dedo	Ponte ungüento y una curita.
lastimarse la muñeca al jugar al volibol	
caerse y lastimarse el brazo	
quemarse la cara con el sol	
me duele la garganta (*present tense*)	

TASK 2 Now, ask your partner what happened to him or her. When your partner tells you what happened, reply by commenting on how the injury looks now (use the words in parentheses). Then, choose advice from the chart that best suits his or her ailment. Hint: One of his or her ailments doesn't involve an injury specific to a body part.

Parte del cuerpo	Consejos
los muslos (hinchados)	No comas y tómate una aspirina.
la cabeza (hinchada)	Estírate antes de jugar al fútbol.
(*no body part*)	Véndate el tobillo y ponte hielo.
los labios (cortados)	Quédate en cama y bebe mucha agua.
el tobillo (torcido)	Ponte hielo y descansa un poco.

Holt Spanish 2 — Activities for Communication

Nombre _____ Clase _____ Fecha _____

¡Mantente en forma!

CAPÍTULO 4

COMMUNICATIVE ACTIVITY 2B

SITUATION You and your neighbor (your partner) have just gotten back from disastrous weekend trips. You both are in really bad physical shape.

TASK 1 Your partner is a physical wreck! Ask your partner what happened to him or her. When your partner tells you what happened, reply by commenting on how the injury looks now (use the words in parentheses). Then, choose advice from the chart that best suits his or her ailment.

MODELO   A — ¿Qué te pasó en el dedo?
B — Me corté.
A — ¡Ahora lo tienes infectado! Ponte ungüento y una curita.

Parte del cuerpo	Consejos
el dedo (infectado)	Ponte un sombrero y no salgas afuera.
la muñeca (torcida)	¡Ten más cuidado!
el brazo (creo que está roto)	No hables tanto y tómate estas pastillas.
la cara (hinchada)	¡Vete al médico!
la garganta (hinchada)	Ponte ungüento y una curita.

TASK 2 Now, answer your partner's questions about what happened to you over the weekend. Listen to his or her advice for each of your ailments. Take notes. Hint: One of your ailments doesn't involve an injury specific to a body part.

¿Qué te pasó?	Consejos
lastimarse los muslos al jugar al fútbol	
darse un golpe en la cabeza con la puerta	
resfriarse ayer	
darse un golpe en la cara y cortarse los labios	
lastimarse el tobillo al caerse	

Holt Spanish 2   Activities for Communication

Copyright © by Holt, Rinehart and Winston All rights reserved

Nombre _____ Clase _____ Fecha _____

Día a día

CAPÍTULO 5

COMMUNICATIVE ACTIVITY 1A

SITUATION You and your sibling (your partner) are responsible for doing certain things around the house before you and your family go on a weekend trip.

TASK 1 Ask your partner if he or she remembered to do the following things. Take notes. If your partner forgot, tell him or her not to worry. You can do it now.

MODELO A — ¿Te acordaste de darle de comer al gato?
    B — Ay, se me olvidó por completo.
    A — No te preocupes. Yo puedo darle de comer ahora.

Los quehaceres	Sí	No
darle de comer al gato		X
sacar la basura		
lavar los platos		
apagar la luz de tu cuarto		
cerrar el garaje		
agarrar el impermeable		

TASK 2 Now, switch roles. Tell your sibling (your partner) whether you have done each of the things he or she asks you about.

Holt Spanish 2

Activities for Communication

Copyright © by Holt, Rinehart and Winston All rights reserved

Nombre _____ Clase _____ Fecha _____

CAPÍTULO 5

Día a día

COMMUNICATIVE ACTIVITY 1B

SITUATION You and your sibling (your partner) are responsible for doing certain things around the house before you and your family go on a weekend trip.

TASK 1 Tell your partner whether you have done each of the things he or she asks you about.

MODELO   A — ¿Te acordaste de darle de comer al gato?
B — Ay, se me olvidó por completo.
A — No te preocupes. Yo puedo darle de comer ahora.

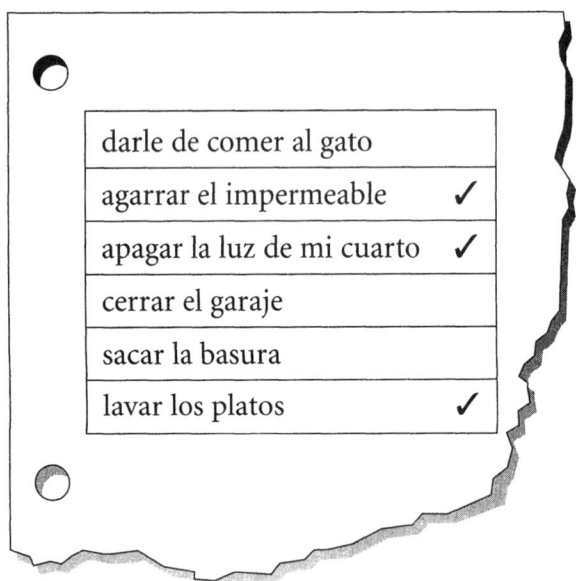

darle de comer al gato	
agarrar el impermeable	✓
apagar la luz de mi cuarto	✓
cerrar el garaje	
sacar la basura	
lavar los platos	✓

TASK 2 Now, switch roles. Ask your sibling (your partner) if he or she remembered to do the following things. Take notes. If your partner forgot, tell him or her not to worry. You can do it now.

Los quehaceres	Sí	No
darle de comer al perro		
recoger los útiles escolares		
apagar la televisión		
cerrar la puerta con llave		
agarrar las llaves		

Holt Spanish 2   Activities for Communication

Nombre _____ Clase _____ Fecha _____

Día a día

CAPÍTULO 5

COMMUNICATIVE ACTIVITY 2A

SITUATION You and your cousin (your partner) are talking about what gifts to get each other's families for the holidays.

TASK 1 Ask your cousin if the members of his or her family are still doing the activities they did last year. Take notes.

MODELO A — ¿Tu madre sigue tejiendo?
B — No, estos días ella pasa mucho tiempo haciendo ejercicio.

La familia	El año pasado	Ahora
madre	tejer	hace ejercicio
hermano Juan	trabajar en mecánica	
hermana Carlota	coleccionar monedas	
hermana Isabel	jugar naipes	
tía María	pintar	
padre	practicar artes marciales	

TASK 2 Now, switch roles. Tell your cousin if the people in your family are still doing what they did last year. If they aren't, tell him or her what they are doing these days.

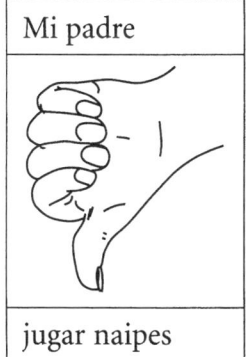

Mi padre — jugar naipes

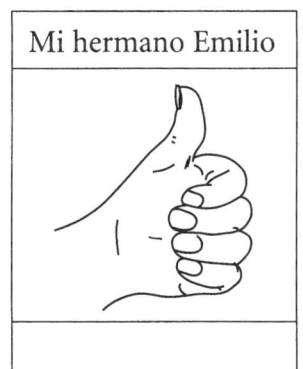

Mi hermano Emilio

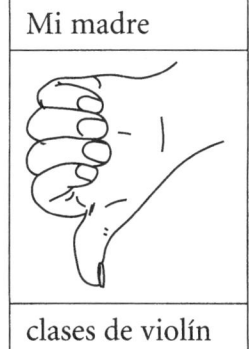

Mi madre — clases de violín

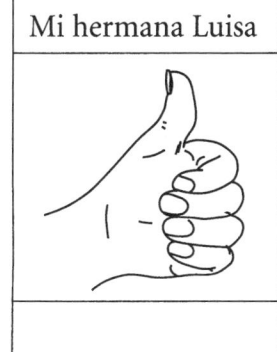

Mi hermana Luisa

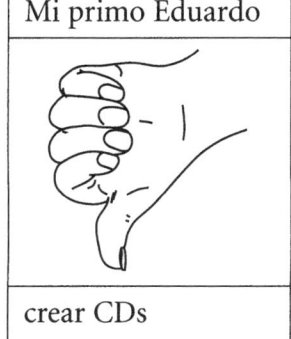

Mi primo Eduardo — crear CDs

Holt Spanish 2   Activities for Communication

Nombre _____ Clase _____ Fecha _____

CAPÍTULO 5

Día a día

COMMUNICATIVE ACTIVITY 2B

SITUATION You and your cousin (your partner) are talking about what gifts to get each other's families for the holidays.

TASK 1 Tell your cousin if the people in your family are still doing what they did last year. If they aren't, tell him or her what they are doing these days.

MODELO   A — ¿Tu madre sigue tejiendo?
B — No, estos días ella pasa mucho tiempo haciendo ejercicio.

Mi madre	Mi hermana Carlota	Mi hermano Juan
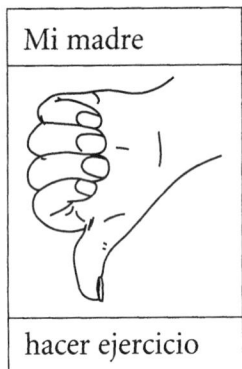	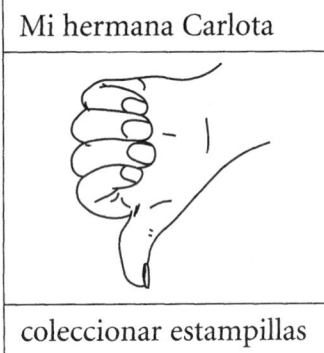	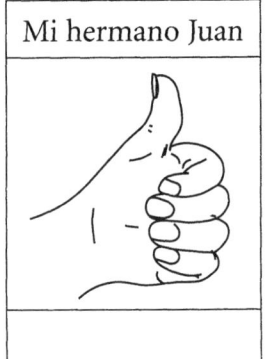
hacer ejercicio	coleccionar estampillas	

Mi tía María	Mi hermana Isabel	Mi padre
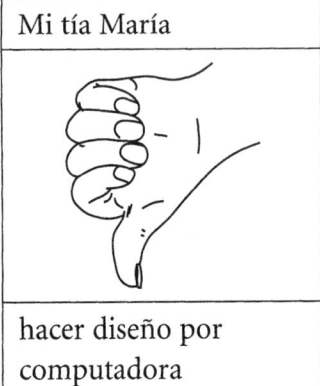	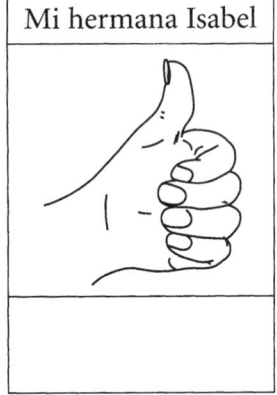	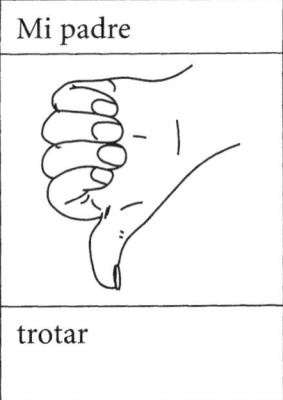
hacer diseño por computadora		trotar

TASK 2 Now, switch roles. Ask your cousin if the members of his or her family are still doing the activities they did last year. Take notes.

La familia	El año pasado	Ahora
madre	tomar clases de guitarra	
padre	coleccionar estampillas	
hermano Emilio	practicar deportes	
hermana Luisa	hacer crucigramas	
primo Eduardo	diseñar páginas Web	

Holt Spanish 2   Activities for Communication

Nombre _____ Clase _____ Fecha _____

Recuerdos

CAPÍTULO 6

COMMUNICATIVE ACTIVITY 1A

SITUATION Your uncle Oliver (your partner) sent you some old family photos of when he and your father were young. However, he forgot to write on them who everyone is, and you don't recognize anyone. You're talking on the phone with him to find out who the people in the pictures are.

TASK 1 Ask your partner who used to do each of the activities in the pictures. Write their names under the correct picture.

MODELO A — ¿Quién siempre sacaba buenas notas?
B — Tu padre siempre sacaba buenas notas.

Mi padre

_____ _____ _____ _____ _____

TASK 2 Now switch roles. Your uncle has some photos of you and your cousins, whom he's never met. Help him figure out who everyone is by answering his questions, using the information in the following chart.

¿Quién?	Siempre...
Mi primo Juan y mi prima Lupe	pelearse
Mi primo Toño	comer pastel
Mi hermano Quique	hacer travesuras
Mis hermanos Eduardo y Lina	contarse chistes
Mis primos José y Carlos	jugar con bloques

Holt Spanish 2

Activities for Communication

Nombre _____ Clase _____ Fecha _____

Recuerdos

CAPÍTULO 6

COMMUNICATIVE ACTIVITY 1B

SITUATION You sent some photos of you and your siblings when you were young to your niece or nephew (your partner), but forgot to write who everyone is. Your partner doesn't recognize anyone when they were young.

TASK 1 Answer your partner's questions about the photos using the information in the chart.

MODELO A — ¿Quién siempre sacaba buenas notas?
B — Tu padre siempre sacaba buenas notas.

Tu padre

¿Quién?	Siempre...
Tu padre	sacar buenas notas
Mi primo Jorge	coleccionar láminas
Yo	trepar a los árboles
Mi prima Elisa	saltar a la cuerda
Tu abuela Emilia y mi primo Tito	jugar a las damas
Mi hermano Francisco	hablar por teléfono

TASK 2 Now, switch roles. Ask your niece or nephew (your partner) who used to do each of the activities. Write their names under the correct pictures.

_____ _____ _____ _____ _____

Holt Spanish 2

Activities for Communication

Recuerdos

CAPÍTULO 6

COMMUNICATIVE ACTIVITY 2A

SITUATION You are part of the welcoming committee for students who have just moved to your town and are new to your school. To get to know one of the new students (your partner), try to find out about his or her life before he or she moved.

TASK 1 Ask your partner what each of these people was like in his or her old town. Then ask your partner to describe what there was in each of the corresponding places, according to the chart. Take notes so that you can tell others about his or her life.

MODELO A — ¿Cómo era el profesor de español?
B — Era muy paciente.
A — ¿Qué había en el salón de la clase de español?
B — Había muchas computadoras.

Las personas	Era...	Los sitios	Había...
El profesor de español	*muy paciente.*	el salón de clase	*muchas computadoras.*
El dentista		la clínica	
La peluquera		la peluquería	
El entrenador		el centro recreativo	
La secretaria del colegio		las oficinas del colegio	

TASK 2 Now your partner wants to know what his or her new town was like for you this past year. Answer your partner's questions by describing the people and places in your life, making logical selections from the chart below.

Las personas	Los sitios
solitario	paredes blancas
bondadoso	unas plantas
cómico	muchas sillas amarillas
estrictos	un televisor pequeño
conversadora	tres estufas y cuatro fregaderos

Nombre _____ Clase _____ Fecha _____

CAPÍTULO 6

Recuerdos

COMMUNICATIVE ACTIVITY 2B

SITUATION You are one of the new kids at school and you have been met by a welcoming committee member (your partner). To get to know you, he or she wants to know all about life in your old town.

TASK 1 Answer your partner's questions by describing the people and places in your old town making logical selections from the chart below.

MODELO A — ¿Cómo era el profesor de español?
B — Era muy paciente.
A — ¿Qué había en el salón de la clase de español?
B — Había muchas computadoras.

Las personas	Los sitios
paciente	muchas computadoras
aventurero	miles de pesas
callado	unos cuadros muy bonitos
chismosa	veinte secadoras
chistoso	un sillón muy cómodo

TASK 2 Now, switch roles. Ask your partner what these people in town were like last year and what there was in each of the corresponding places, according to the chart. Take notes so that you can recognize the people and places later.

Las personas	Era...	Los sitios	Había...
El profesor de inglés		el salón de clase	
El conductor del autobús		la estación de autobuses	
La cocinera del colegio		la cafetería	
Los policías del pueblo		la comisaría	
El banquero		el banco	

Holt Spanish 2 — Activities for Communication

Nombre _____ Clase _____ Fecha _____

¡Buen provecho!

CAPÍTULO 7

COMMUNICATIVE ACTIVITY 1A

SITUATION You're eating out at an authentic Caribbean restaurant with your dad, who doesn't speak any Spanish. Your waiter doesn't speak any English. Help your dad figure out what to order.

TASK 1 Ask the waiter how each of the dishes tastes today. Take notes.

MODELO A — ¿Qué tal está el gazpacho?
B — Hoy está un poco aguado. No se lo recomiendo.

El menú	Hoy...	Recomendación
Gazpacho	aguado	
Caldo de pollo		
Pollo asado con gandules		
Bistec encebollado		
Flan de vainilla		
Fresas con crema		
Sopa de fideos		

TASK 2 Now switch roles. Your partner has to determine what his or her dad would like to eat. Answer the questions about today's dishes choosing from the information in the box. Make a personal recommendation.

La comida hoy...
perfecto(a)   fresco(a)
exquisito(a)   le falta sal
sabroso(a)   le falta sabor
echado(a) a perder   rico(a)

Holt Spanish 2
Activities for Communication

Nombre _____ Clase _____ Fecha _____

CAPÍTULO

¡Buen provecho!

COMMUNICATIVE ACTIVITY 1B

SITUATION You're the waiter at an authentic Caribbean restaurant. Your client must help his or her dad figure out what to order.

TASK 1 Answer your partner's questions about today's dishes choosing from the information in the box. Then make a personal recommendation.

MODELO A — ¿Qué tal está el gazpacho?
B — Hoy está un poco aguado. No se lo recomiendo.

La comida hoy...

aguado(a)   quemado(a)
exquisito(a)   rico(a)
sabroso(a)   en su punto
echado(a) a perder   perfecto(a)

TASK 2 Now switch roles. Help your dad decide what to eat by asking the waiter how each of the dishes in the chart tastes today. Take notes.

El menú	Hoy...	Recomendación
Ensalada mixta		
Caldo de pollo		
Chuleta de cerdo		
Bistec encebollado		
Café		
Agua mineral		

Holt Spanish 2 — Activities for Communication

Nombre _____ Clase _____ Fecha _____

¡Buen provecho!

CAPÍTULO 7

COMMUNICATIVE ACTIVITY 2A

SITUATION You and your brother or sister are preparing a birthday meal for your mother. Your sibling hasn't helped you at all.

TASK 1 Remind your brother or sister what he or she was doing while you were working hard. Listen to his or her response and then say that each chore is done.

MODELO   A — ¡Tú veías la televisión mientras yo cortaba toda la lechuga!
B — Te dije que quería ver la televisión.
A — Pues, la lechuga está cortada.

Tu hermano(a)	Tú
ver la televisión	cortar la lechuga
hablar por teléfono	hervir los mariscos
jugar videojuegos	picar el ajo
hacer la tarea	cocinar las verduras
arreglarse	freír las chuletas

TASK 2 Now switch roles. Your brother or sister is doing all the work and you're not helping with the meal! Listen as your sibling tells you what you were doing while he or she was working and respond with your activities in the chart.

Las actividades
tener que jugar al fútbol
necesitar arreglar el cuarto
deber estudiar toda la tarde
querer hablar con tu amigo
ir a trotar en el parque

Holt Spanish 2   Activities for Communication

Nombre _____ Clase _____ Fecha _____

¡Buen provecho!

CAPÍTULO 7

COMMUNICATIVE ACTIVITY 2B

TASK 1 You and your brother or sister are preparing a birthday meal for your mother. You haven't helped at all with the chores.

TASK 1 Listen as your sibling says what you were doing while he or she was hard at work. Respond by telling him or her what you said you planned to do using the activities in the chart.

MODELO A — ¡Tú veías la televisión mientras yo cortaba toda la lechuga!
B — Te dije que quería ver la televisión.
A — Pues, la lechuga está cortada.

Las actividades
querer ver la televisión
necesitar hablar por teléfono
ir a jugar a videojuegos
tener que hacer la tarea
deber arreglarse

TASK 2 Now switch roles. Remind your brother or sister what he or she was doing while you were working hard. Listen to his or her response and then say that each chore is done.

Tu hermano(a)	Tú
jugar al fútbol	preparar el postre
arreglar el cuarto	hornear el pollo
estudiar toda la tarde	freír las cebollas
hablar con su amigo	derretir la mantequilla
trotar en el parque	limpiar la cocina

Holt Spanish 2   Activities for Communication

Nombre _____ Clase _____ Fecha _____

Tiendas y puestos

CAPÍTULO 8

COMMUNICATIVE ACTIVITY 1A

SITUATION You and your partner are shopping for clothes for a big party.

TASK 1 Ask your partner, who is in the dressing room, how each of the following items fits. Take notes. Look at your notes and make a list of what your partner should buy.

MODELO A — ¿Cómo te quedan los zapatos?
            B — La verdad es que me quedan un poco apretados.

La ropa	¿Cómo te queda(n)?
los zapatos	un poco apretados
el cinturón	
la corbata	
el traje	
la camisa roja	
la camiseta verde	
los pantalones negros	

TASK 2 Now, switch roles. Choose from the following expressions to answer your partner's questions about how each of the clothing items fits. Use each expression at least once.

quedar (muy / poco) apretado
quedar (muy / poco) flojo
quedar elegante
(no) hacer juego
(no) sentar bien

Holt Spanish 2 — Activities for Communication

Nombre _____ Clase _____ Fecha _____

Tiendas y puestos

CAPÍTULO 8

COMMUNICATIVE ACTIVITY 1B

SITUATION You and your partner are shopping for clothes for a big party.

TASK 1 You are in the dressing room trying on lots of clothing. Choose from the following expressions to answer your partner's questions about how each item fits. Use each expression at least once.

MODELO A — ¿Cómo te quedan los zapatos?
B — La verdad es que me quedan un poco apretados.

| quedar (muy / poco) apretado |
| quedar (muy / poco) flojo |
| quedar elegante |
| (no) hacer juego |
| (no) sentar bien |

TASK 2 Now, switch roles. Ask your partner, who is in the dressing room, how each of the following items fits. Take notes. Look at your notes and make a list of what your partner should buy.

La ropa	¿Cómo te queda(n)?
la minifalda	
la bufanda roja	
los guantes	
la falda a media pierna	
el traje de baño	
el cinturón	

Holt Spanish 2 — Activities for Communication

Nombre _____ Clase _____ Fecha _____

CAPÍTULO 8

Tiendas y puestos

COMMUNICATIVE ACTIVITY 2A

SITUATION It's your last day in Santiago and you still haven't bought anything for your best friend. You are at the city's largest open air market.

TASK 1 Ask the vendor (your partner) how much each of the pictured items costs. Then bargain with him or her about a specific item as indicated in the box. Take notes of the best prices. After bargaining for all the items, purchase the best deal for your friend.

MODELO A — ¿Cuánto cuestan los tejidos?
B — Le voy a dar un precio especial. Se los doy por treinta y cinco mil pesos cada uno.
A — ¿Me puede rebajar el precio de ese tejido pequeño?
B — Bueno, mi última oferta es treinta mil pesos.

el tejido pequeño 30.000 pesos

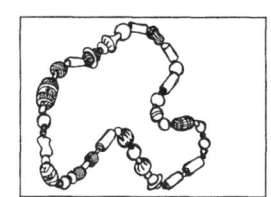

collares de plata    cerámicas de barro    cestas de paja

TASK 2 Now, switch roles. You are the vendor. Tell the client (your partner) the special price indicated for each item. Then offer him or her a final sale price.

Los artículos	El precio especial	La última oferta
las joyas	45.200 pesos	
las cerámicas	37.000 pesos	
los artículos de cuero	82.500 pesos	

Holt Spanish 2   Activities for Communication

Nombre _____ Clase _____ Fecha _____

Tiendas y puestos

CAPÍTULO 8

COMMUNICATIVE ACTIVITY 2B

SITUATION You are a vendor at Santiago's largest open air market. It's the last day of the week and you are anxious to sell your merchandise.

TASK 1 Tell your client (your partner) a special price, as indicated in the chart below, for each item that he or she asks about. Then offer your partner a final sale price.

MODELO
A — ¿Cuánto cuestan los tejidos?
B — Le voy a dar un precio especial. Se los doy por treinta y cinco mil pesos cada uno.
A — ¿Me puede rebajar el precio de ese tejido pequeño?
B — Bueno, mi última oferta es treinta mil pesos.

el tejido pequeño 30.000 pesos

Los artículos	El precio especial	La última oferta
las pinturas	50.000 pesos	40.000 pesos
los collares	125.000 pesos	
las cerámicas	55.000 pesos	
las cestas	23.500 pesos	

TASK 2 Now, switch roles. Ask the vendor (your partner) how much each of the pictured items costs. Then bargain with him or her about a specific item as indicated in the box. Take notes of the best prices. After bargaining for all of the items, purchase the best deal for your friend.

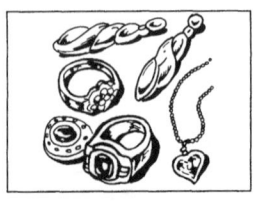

joyas de oro    cerámicas de barro 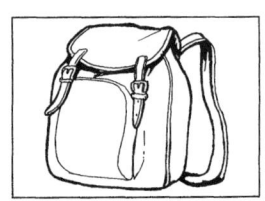   mochilas de cuero

_____   _____   _____

Holt Spanish 2   Activities for Communication

Copyright © by Holt, Rinehart and Winston   All rights reserved   32

Nombre _____ Clase _____ Fecha _____

A nuestro alrededor

CAPÍTULO 9

COMMUNICATIVE ACTIVITY 1A

SITUATION You and your partner are camping in the desert and have each returned from separate hikes.

TASK 1 Tell your partner that you were walking along and saw various things from the chart. Tell him or her how you reacted, using the corresponding verb.

MODELO A — Sí, caminaba tranquilamente cuando vi un río.
B — ¿Pasaste por el río?
A — No, doblé a la derecha.

Vi...	Yo...
un río	doblar a la derecha
muchos cactus	evitar
un águila	sacar fotos
un pájaro rojo	mirar
una serpiente	decidir huir
un lagarto	tocar
un lobo	gritar por ayuda

TASK 2 Now, switch roles. When your partner tells you what he or she saw, ask a logical question about his or her reaction, using the verbs in the chart. Write what your partner saw in the left-hand column. Listen to his or her answer, and take notes on what happened.

Viste...	¿Tú...?	Tú...
	tocar	
	evitar	
	correr	
	llorar	
	gritar por ayuda	
	enfrentar	

Holt Spanish 2 — Activities for Communication

Nombre _____ Clase _____ Fecha _____

A nuestro alrededor

CAPÍTULO 9

COMMUNICATIVE ACTIVITY 1B

SITUATION You and your partner are camping in the desert and have each returned from separate hikes.

TASK 1 When your partner tells you what he or she saw, ask a logical question about his or her reaction, using the verbs in the chart. Write what your partner saw in the left-hand column. Listen to his or her answer, and take notes on what happened.

MODELO   A — Sí, caminaba tranquilamente cuando vi un río.
         B — ¿Pasaste por el río?
         A — No, doblé a la derecha.

Viste...	¿Tú...?	Tú...
un río	pasar por	doblaste a la derecha
	tocar	
	correr	
	evitar	
	enfrentar	
	gritar por ayuda	
	llorar	

TASK 2 Now, switch roles. Tell your partner what you saw and how you reacted, using the corresponding verb in the chart.

Vi...	Yo...
una piedra grande	subir
los cactus	tocar
un buitre	enfrentar
una serpiente	decidir huir
un búho	sacar fotos
un oso	evitar

Holt Spanish 2   Activities for Communication

Nombre _____ Clase _____ Fecha _____

A nuestro alrededor

CAPÍTULO 9

COMMUNICATIVE ACTIVITY 2A

SITUATION You and your sibling (your partner) are comparing agendas for your week at a luxury resort.

TASK 1 Using the future tense, ask your partner what he or she will do each day of the vacation. Take notes. Then, use the corresponding verb to say how you hope it turns out.

MODELO A — ¿Qué harás el miércoles?
 B — Volaré con ala delta.
 A — ¡Espero que no haga mucho viento!

Día de la semana	¿Qué hará?	Espero que...
el lunes		haber muchos peces
el martes		(tú) llevar la linterna
el miércoles	volará con ala delta	no hacer mucho viento
el jueves		(tú) ver una ballena
el viernes		no llover
el sábado		no ser aburrido

TASK 2 Now, switch roles. Using the future tense, tell your partner what you are going to do each day.

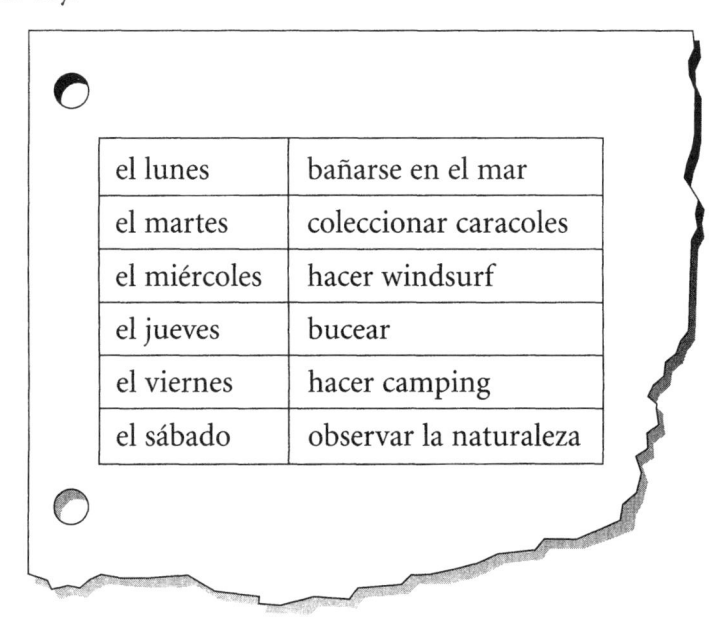

el lunes	bañarse en el mar
el martes	coleccionar caracoles
el miércoles	hacer windsurf
el jueves	bucear
el viernes	hacer camping
el sábado	observar la naturaleza

Holt Spanish 2 Activities for Communication

Nombre _____ Clase _____ Fecha _____

A nuestro alrededor

CAPÍTULO 9

COMMUNICATIVE ACTIVITY 2B

SITUATION You and your sibling (your partner) are comparing agendas for your week at a luxury resort.

TASK 1 Using the future tense, tell your partner what you are going to do each day.

MODELO A — ¿Qué harás el miércoles?
 B — Volaré con ala delta.
 A — ¡Espero que no haga mucho viento!

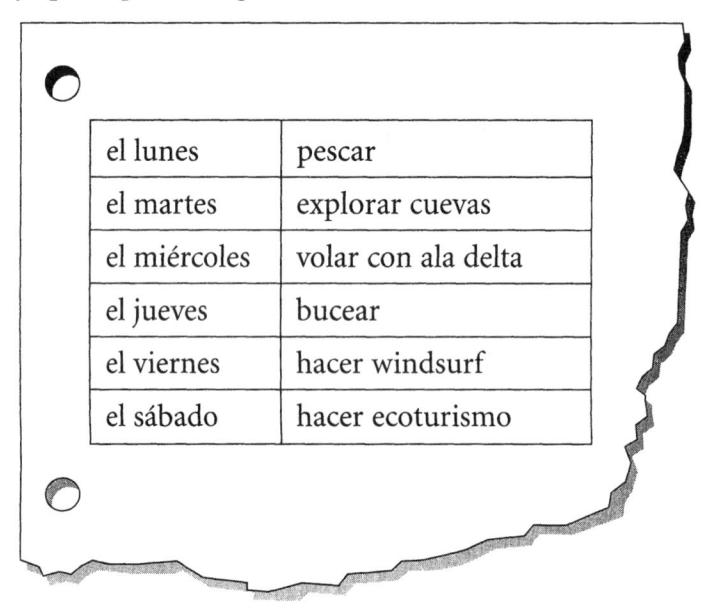

el lunes	pescar
el martes	explorar cuevas
el miércoles	volar con ala delta
el jueves	bucear
el viernes	hacer windsurf
el sábado	hacer ecoturismo

TASK 2 Now, switch roles. Using the future tense, ask your partner what he or she will do each day of the vacation. Take notes. Then, use the corresponding verb to say how you hope it turns out.

Día de la semana	¿Qué hará?	Espero que...
el lunes		(tú) ponerse crema protectora
el martes		(tú) encontrar uno bonito
el miércoles		no haber olas grandes
el jueves		(tú) ver una ballena
el viernes		(tú) no enfrentar un oso
el sábado		ser divertido

Holt Spanish 2   Activities for Communication

Nombre _____ Clase _____ Fecha _____

De vacaciones

CAPÍTULO 10

COMMUNICATIVE ACTIVITY 1A

SITUATION You have to be at the Buenos Aires airport by noon, but you want to do some last-minute sightseeing. You are out of cash, but you have your credit card. You are in the tourist office to find out when various tourist attractions are open and if they accept credit cards.

TASK 1 Ask your partner (a tourist office employee) what time the following places open. Then, find out if you can use your credit card to pay at each place.

MODELO
A — ¿Sabe usted a qué hora abre el Museo de Arte Moderno?
B — Sí, abre a las diez y media.
A — Disculpe, ¿se puede pagar la entrada con tarjeta de crédito?
B — No, sólo se puede pagar con dinero en efectivo.

Los lugares turísticos	Abre...	¿Tarjeta de crédito?	
		sí	no
el Museo de Arte Moderno	10:00 AM		X
el palacio San Martín			
la casa de Carlos Gardel			
el café Internet Mundi			
la Catedral Metropolitana			
la Casa Rosada			

TASK 2 Now switch roles. You work at the information desk of the tourist office in Buenos Aires. Use the information in the chart to tell your partner (a tourist) what time each place opens. Then, answer his or her questions about what methods of payment are accepted at each place.

Los lugares turísticos	Abre...	Se puede pagar...
el Palacio Barolo	11:30 AM	sólo con dinero en efectivo
la Torre de los ingleses	10:45 AM	con dinero en efectivo o con cheques de viajero
el Museo de Ciencias Naturales	8:15 AM	con dinero en efectivo o con tarjeta de crédito
el Café Tortoni	11:00 AM	con dinero en efectivo, con tarjeta de crédito o con cheques de viajero
la basílica de San Francisco	9:30 AM	con dinero en efectivo o con cheques de viajero

Holt Spanish 2   Activities for Communication

Nombre _____ Clase _____ Fecha _____

De vacaciones

CAPÍTULO 10

COMMUNICATIVE ACTIVITY 1B

SITUATION You work at the information desk of the tourist office in Buenos Aires.

TASK 1 Use the information in the chart to tell your partner (a tourist) what time each place opens. Then answer his or her questions about what methods of payment are accepted at each place. Take notes.

MODELO   A — ¿Sabe usted a qué hora abre el Museo de Arte Moderno?
B — Sí, abre a las diez y media.
A — Disculpe, ¿se puede pagar la entrada con tarjeta de crédito?
B — No, sólo se puede pagar con dinero en efectivo.

Los lugares turísticos	Abre...	Se puede pagar...
el Museo de Arte Moderno	10:00 AM	sólo con dinero en efectivo
el palacio San Martín	9:45 AM	con dinero en efectivo o con cheques de viajero
la casa de Carlos Gardel	11:15 AM	con tarjeta de crédito, con dinero en efectivo o con cheques de viajero
el café Internet Mundi	8:30 AM	sólo con dinero en efectivo
la Catedral Metropolitana	9:30 AM	con dinero en efectivo o con cheques de viajero
la Casa Rosada	9:00 AM	con tarjeta de crédito, con dinero en efectivo o con cheques de viajero

TASK 2 Now switch roles. You have to be at the Buenos Aires airport by noon, but you want to do some last-minute sightseeing. You are out of cash and you lost your credit card, but you still have some traveler's checks. Ask your partner (a tourist office employee) what time the following places open. Then, find out if you can use traveler's checks to pay at each place. Take notes.

Los lugares turísticos	Abre...	¿Cheques de viajero?	
		sí	no
el Palacio Barolo			
la Torre de los ingleses			
el Museo de Ciencias Naturales			
el Café Tortoni			
la basílica de San Francisco			

Holt Spanish 2

Activities for Communication

De vacaciones

CAPÍTULO 10

COMMUNICATIVE ACTIVITY 2A

SITUATION You and your friend (your partner) are talking on the phone about where everyone is this summer.

TASK 1 Ask your friend (your partner) if he or she has any news about the people in the chart. Say that you can't believe the news. Take notes on where everyone is and what each person is probably doing.

MODELO A — ¿Qué noticias tienes de Javier?
B — No lo vas a creer, pero está en Perú.
A — ¡No me digas!
B — Estará explorando la selva.

Los amigos	¿Dónde está(n)?	¿Qué estará(n) haciendo?
Javier	Perú	Estará explorando la selva.
Ana Elisa		
Juan Pablo		
Carmen y Sandra		
Alberto		
Lourdes y Lola		

TASK 2 Tell your friend where everyone is. Using the future tense of the verb **estar** with a present participle, say what they are probably doing.

Los amigos	Está(n) en...	Estará(n)...
Eduardo	México	subir un volcán
Eva y Antonio	España	hospedarse en un castillo
Gabriel	Miami	tomar un crucero
Leticia y Andrés	Santo Domingo	saltar en paracaídas
Daniel	Chile	bañarse en las aguas termales

Nombre _____ Clase _____ Fecha _____

CAPÍTULO 10

De vacaciones

COMMUNICATIVE ACTIVITY 2B

SITUATION You and your friend (your partner) are talking on the phone about where everyone is this summer.

TASK 1 Tell your friend where everyone is. Use the future tense of the verb **estar** with a present participle to say what they are probably doing.

MODELO A — ¿Qué noticias tienes de Javier?
B — No lo vas a creer, pero está en Perú.
A — ¡No me digas!
B — Estará explorando la selva.

Los amigos	Está(n) en...	Estará(n)...
Javier	Perú	explorar la selva
Ana Elisa	Argentina	hacer un tour de Buenos Aires
Juan Pablo	Puerto Rico	comprar recuerdos
Carmen y Sandra	Florida	visitar el parque nacional Everglades
Alberto	Costa Rica	ver una catarata
Lourdes y Lola	Texas	hacer senderismo en el desierto

TASK 2 Ask your friend (your partner) if he or she has any news about the people in the chart. Say that you can't believe the news. Take notes on where everyone is and what each person is probably doing.

Los amigos	¿Dónde está(n)?	¿Qué estará(n) haciendo?
Eduardo		
Eva y Antonio		
Gabriel		
Leticia y Andrés		
Daniel		

Holt Spanish 2 — Activities for Communication

Picture Sequences

Familiares y amigos

CAPÍTULO 1

PICTURE SEQUENCES

Two teenagers are about to embark on two very different adventures. With a partner, create a conversation based on what you see in each scene below.

Nombre _____ Clase _____ Fecha _____

En el vecindario

CAPÍTULO 2

PICTURE SEQUENCES

It's career day at school and two students have brought guest speakers to class. Later the two students are at home. With a partner, say what is taking place in each scene below.

Holt Spanish 2

Activities for Communication

Copyright © by Holt, Rinehart and Winston All rights reserved

Nombre _____ Clase _____ Fecha _____

Pueblos y ciudades

CAPÍTULO 3

PICTURE SEQUENCES

A girl and her family are on vacation in a small town. Her mother asks her to run some errands. With a partner, create a conversation for each scene below.

Holt Spanish 2

Activities for Communication

Copyright © by Holt, Rinehart and Winston All rights reserved

Nombre _____ Clase _____ Fecha _____

¡Mantente en forma!

CAPÍTULO 4

PICTURE SEQUENCES

Two friends recount their troubled weekend to each other. With a partner, create a conversation for the scenes below.

Holt Spanish 2 — Activities for Communication

Nombre _____ Clase _____ Fecha _____

Día a día

CAPÍTULO 5

PICTURE SEQUENCES

You and your friend are almost complete opposites. With a partner create a conversation based on the following scenes describing what each of you is interested in doing.

Nombre _____ Clase _____ Fecha _____

Recuerdos

CAPÍTULO 6

PICTURE SEQUENCES

A couple of years ago you and your family moved to Mexico. With a partner, create a conversation remembering what you used to do when you were younger, how you reacted when you found out that you were moving, and what your new home and friends were like.

Holt Spanish 2

Activities for Communication

Nombre _____ Clase _____ Fecha _____

¡Buen provecho!

CAPÍTULO 7

PICTURE SEQUENCES

Last week you got your first paycheck from your new job. To celebrate you took your parents out to eat. In groups of three create a conversation describing what happened.

Nombre _____ Clase _____ Fecha _____

CAPÍTULO 8

Tiendas y puestos

PICTURE SEQUENCES

You are really getting good at bargaining at the market. With a partner, create a conversation describing what happened yesterday when you saw a necklace you liked.

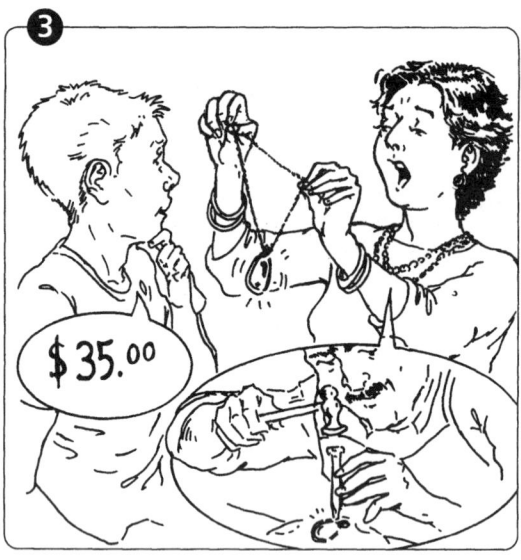

Nombre _____ Clase _____ Fecha _____

A nuestro alrededor

CAPÍTULO 9

PICTURE SEQUENCES

Your mother has just told you that she won a big trip for the whole family. In groups of three, create a conversation describing what each person hopes the vacation will be like and what the final destination will be according to your mother.

Nombre _____ Clase _____ Fecha _____

De vacaciones

CAPÍTULO 10

PICTURE SEQUENCES

Two teenagers are talking to each other about their plans for this summer. With a partner, create a conversation based on what you see in each scene below.

Holt Spanish 2

Activities for Communication

Interpersonal Communication Cards

Nombre _____ Clase _____ Fecha _____

Familiares y amigos

CAPÍTULO 1

INTERPERSONAL COMMUNICATION: INTERVIEWS

Vocabulario 1/Gramática 1

I am a journalist for TeenFit magazine. I have passed out a survey on the health habits of junior high and high school students. Respond to my questions.

¿Cuántos años tienes?

¿A qué hora te acuestas cada noche?

¿Cómo te mantienes en forma?

¿Qué haces todas las mañanas?

¿Qué haces los fines de semana?

Vocabulario 2/Gramática 2

Imagine that you've earned a trip to Mexico City for having perfect attendance this year at school. I am a friend helping you get ready for the trip. Respond to my questions.

Antes de ir al aeropuerto, ¿qué debes hacer?

¿Quién está haciendo las maletas?

¿Puedo ayudarte?

¿Adónde piensas ir en la ciudad?

¿Prefieres la comida o la cultura de México?

Repaso

Imagine that you are going on a trip to your favorite vacation destination to visit one of your aunts. Answer my questions.

¿Adónde vas a ir?

¿Cómo es tu tía?

¿Qué te gusta hacer con ella?

¿Qué piensas hacer en _____?

Antes de irte, ¿qué debes hacer?

Holt Spanish 2

Activities for Communication

Nombre _____ Clase _____ Fecha _____

CAPÍTULO 1

Familiares y amigos

INTERPERSONAL COMMUNICATION: ROLE-PLAYS

Vocabulario 1/Gramática 1

STUDENT A You just met **Student B**. Introduce yourselves. Then ask **Student B** what he or she is like and what he or she likes to do. Also ask what **Student B**'s best friend is like. Then, introduce a friend to **Student B**. Now, answer **Student B**'s questions.

STUDENT B You and **Student A** just met. Introduce yourselves. Then answer **Student A**'s questions about you and your best friend. Now, ask **Student A** similar questions. What is **Student A** like and what does he or she like to do? Also, ask **Student A** what he or she does on weekends.

Vocabulario 2/Gramática 2

STUDENT A You and **Student B** are planning what to do this afternoon. Ask **Student B** what he or she wants to do. Listen to **Student B**'s suggestions. Then, decide where you are going to go. Listen to what **Student B** says. Offer to help him or her.

STUDENT B You and **Student A** are making plans for this afternoon. Listen to **Student A**. Then tell him or her that you feel like going to the movies or going to the mall. Decide what you are going to do. Tell **Student A** that first you have to clean your room.

Repaso

STUDENT A **Student B** is a new employee for a cleaning service where you work. Introduce yourself to **Student B**. Tell **Student B** to please take out the trash and clean the bathroom. Answer **Student B**'s questions by telling him or her to vacuum the office floor and to wash the dishes in the kitchen.

STUDENT B Imagine that you are a new employee at a cleaning service. Greet **Student A**. Listen to the instructions given by **Student A**. Then ask **Student A** what else you have to do and what needs to be done in the kitchen.

Holt Spanish 2
Activities for Communication

Nombre _____ Clase _____ Fecha _____

En el vecindario

CAPÍTULO 2

INTERPERSONAL COMMUNICATION: INTERVIEWS

Vocabulario 1/Gramática 1

Imagine that you and your parents have just moved to a new neighborhood. You have gotten to know the Flores and Ortega families before your parents have. Respond to the following questions.

¿De dónde son los Flores y los Ortega?

¿Qué trabajo realiza la señora Ortega?

¿Sabe hablar muchos idiomas?

¿A qué se dedica el señor Flores?

¿Conocen muy bien los Flores a los Ortega?

Vocabulario 2/Gramática 2

I am a friend that has never been to your home before. Respond to my questions.

Descríbeme tu habitación.

¿Dónde está el baño?

¿Qué hay en la sala?

¿Dónde está la cocina?

¿Qué hay en tu habitación?

Repaso

You are a final candidate to be on a home-renovation reality show. I need to find out a bit more about you, your family, and your neighbors before making my final decision. Respond to my questions.

¿De dónde eres tú?

¿Vives en un apartamento o en una casa?

¿A qué se dedican tus padres?

¿Conoces a tus vecinos? ¿Cómo son?

Descríbeme tu casa ideal.

Holt Spanish 2 Activities for Communication

Nombre _____ Clase _____ Fecha _____

¡Empecemos!

CAPÍTULO 2

INTERPERSONAL COMMUNICATION: ROLE-PLAYS

Vocabulario 1/Gramática 1

STUDENT A Imagine that **Student B** is your new neighbor. Introduce yourself to him or her. Then, introduce **Student B** to the following neighbors: a banker, a hair stylist, and a carpenter. Tell **Student B** at least one thing that each of your neighbors knows how to do. Ask what **Student B**'s profession is.

STUDENT B Imagine that you are **Student A**'s new neighbor. Respond to **Student A**'s greeting. Then, say that you are pleased to meet the neighbors that **Student A** introduces you to. Respond to **Student A**'s question by saying that you design Web pages.

Vocabulario 2/Gramática 2

STUDENT A Imagine that you are **Student B**'s parent. Tell him or her that the following things need to be done: feed the dog, dust the furniture, water the plants, and sweep the floor. Listen to **Student B**'s comments after each of your statements.

STUDENT B Imagine that **Student A** is your parent. Listen to him or her tell you what you need to do around the house. After each of **Student A**'s statements, complain that your brother Luis never has to do these things, but also say that you already did one of the chores.

Haz el favor de....   **Hay que...**   **Nunca le toca...**   **Estoy harto(a) de...**

Repaso

STUDENT A You and **Student B** are interested in finding out about each other's home lives. Take turns asking each other about your parents' professions. Ask **Student B** to describe his or her home to you. Then respond to **Student B**'s questions.

STUDENT B You and **Student A** are interested in finding out about each other's home lives. Take turns asking each other about your parents' professions. Then answer **Student A**'s questions. Ask **Student A** similar questions about his or her home.

¿A qué se dedica...?   **Descríbeme...**   **a la derecha de**   **a la izquierda de**

Holt Spanish 2   Activities for Communication
Copyright © by Holt, Rinehart and Winston All rights reserved   58

Nombre _____ Clase _____ Fecha _____

Pueblos y ciudades

CAPÍTULO 3

INTERPERSONAL COMMUNICATION: INTERVIEWS

Vocabulario 1/Gramática 1

Imagine that you just got back from a trip to my hometown. I am eager to find out all that you did. Answer my questions.

Después de llegar, ¿sacaste dinero en el banco?

Diste una vuelta por el parque, ¿verdad?

¿Viste el monumento de Cristóbal Colón?

¿Fuiste a la heladería del pueblo?

¿Te paseaste por el centro? ¿Qué hiciste allí?

Vocabulario 2/Gramática 2

I am an exchange student that has just arrived at your house for a one-month stay. I need help getting around town. Can you help me? When possible, answer my questions using formal commands.

¿Cómo se puede llegar a su casa desde el colegio?

¿Sabe usted dónde está la embajada americana?

¿Qué debo hacer para llegar al supermercado?

¿Qué se vende en una librería?

¿Está la autopista muy cerca de su casa?

Repaso

You are throwing a birthday party for your best friend this evening. I am one of the guests and have called you with some last-minute questions.

¿Ya compraste el pastel de cumpleaños, el helado y el pollo?

¿Dónde compraste todo?

¿Qué diligencias tuviste que hacer?

¿Cómo se puede llegar a tu casa desde el colegio?

¿Me puedes decir si el banco de tu barrio se cierra a las cinco?

Holt Spanish 2

Activities for Communication

Nombre _____ Clase _____ Fecha _____

Pueblos y ciudades

CAPÍTULO 3

INTERPERSONAL COMMUNICATION: ROLE-PLAYS

Vocabulario 1/Gramática 1

STUDENT A You are from a big city and are running errands for your grandmother in Smallville with her dog Spot. Politely ask **Student B** if he or she could tell you where one can buy meat, buy pastries, and buy flowers. Listen to **Student B**'s response, then thank him or her. Switch roles. Answer **Student B**'s questions.

STUDENT B Imagine that you are a citizen of Smallville and **Student A** approaches you with his or her dog. Answer **Student A**'s questions. Tell him or her that dogs are not permitted in any of these shops.

Vocabulario 2/Gramática 2

STUDENT A You are a tourist in a big city and think you are lost. Ask **Student B** if you are going the right way to the Internet café, Coco's. Listen to his or her response. Then, ask **Student B** to repeat what he or she just said. Switch roles.

STUDENT B **Student A** is a tourist and thinks he or she is lost. Listen to **Student A**'s question. Tell **Student A** that he or she is going in the right direction. He or she needs to go straight for two blocks, then turn left at the intersection of 7th Street and Avenue Isabela.

Repaso

STUDENT A You're on vacation and your aunt has given you a list of things to buy. She needs fish, flowers, and bread. You don't know where to buy these things nor where each store is located. Ask **Student B** if he or she can help you.

STUDENT B **Student A** is visiting your town and is running errands. Help **Student A** by telling him or her what stores to go to. Also tell him or her where they are located.

Holt Spanish 2   Activities for Communication

Nombre _____ Clase _____ Fecha _____

¡Mantente en forma!

CAPÍTULO 4

INTERPERSONAL COMMUNICATION: INTERVIEWS

Vocabulario 1/Gramática 1

Imagine that you just finished playing a competitive game of soccer. (You decide whether you have won or lost the game.) I am a sports journalist that has just approached you after the game. Answer my questions.

¿Cómo te sentiste cuando ganaste (perdiste) el partido?

¿Cómo se sintió el otro equipo cuando perdió (ganó)?

¿Qué les dijo el entrenador a ustedes después del partido?

¿Cómo reaccionaron los animadores?

¿Qué tal estuvo el partido de ayer?

Vocabulario 2/Gramática 2

I am a friend of yours and have noticed that you look a bit under the weather. Respond to my questions.

No te veo bien. ¿Estás enfermo(a)?

Te duele la garganta, ¿verdad?

A mí me duele la garganta también. ¿Tienes algún consejo?

¿Qué te pasó ayer cuando te caíste?

¿Te lastimaste algo más?

Repaso

Imagine that you just got back from a tournament in which you participated in many events. I am a friend who is interested in how things turned out for you. Answer my questions.

¿Cómo te fue en gimnasia?

¿Ganaste el partido de básquetbol?

¿Cómo te sentiste cuando ganaste (perdiste)?

Me dijo tu entrenadora que te lastimaste en el partido. ¿Es verdad?

No te veo bien, ¿qué tienes?

Holt Spanish 2 — Activities for Communication

Nombre _____ Clase _____ Fecha _____

¡Mantente en forma!

CAPÍTULO 4

INTERPERSONAL COMMUNICATION: ROLE-PLAYS

Vocabulario 1/Gramática 1

STUDENT A Ask **Student B** how each of the following events turned out: water skiing, track and field, and a basketball game. Listen to **Student B** and ask how he or she felt after each event.

STUDENT B Listen to **Student A**'s questions about the events you took part in. Respond by saying how each event went and whether you won. Tell **Student A** that you won the water skiing and track and field events but you lost the basketball game.

Vocabulario 2/Gramática 2

STUDENT A You and **Student B** are both having bad days. Ask **Student B** what happened to him or her. After each comment, give **Student B** advice on how to improve his or her situation. Now, answer **Student B**'s questions. Your throat, your toe, and your ear hurt.

STUDENT B You and **Student A** are both having bad days. Answer **Student A**'s questions about what has happened to you. You are having problems with your ankle and your wrist, and you have a cold. Listen to **Student A**'s advice. Now, ask **Student A** what's the matter. Give **Student A** advice on how to improve his or her situation.

Repaso

STUDENT A **Student B** has had a horrific day! Ask **Student B** about his or her in-line skating competition and his or her baseball game. How did each event turn out? Respond to his or her comments. Did losing make him or her very sad? Also, tell **Student B** that a friend told you that he or she fell at the game. Did he or she get hurt?

STUDENT B You have had the worst day of your life! You just lost a very important in-line skating tournament and a baseball game. How do you feel about this? Answer **Student A**'s questions.

Holt Spanish 2 Activities for Communication

Nombre _____ Clase _____ Fecha _____

Día a día

CAPÍTULO 5

INTERPERSONAL COMMUNICATION: INTERVIEWS

Vocabulario 1/Gramática 1
Imagine that you are with your host family in Costa Rica for the first time. I am your host mother and would like to know more about your daily routine. Answer my questions.

¿Te duchas por la mañana o por la noche?

¿Tienes que irte temprano a la escuela?

¿Tardas en arreglarte para salir?

¿Te afeitas todos los días?

¿Necesitas ponerte los lentes de contacto todos los días?

Vocabulario 2/Gramática 2
Everyone in your family is extremely musically talented. Your family even has a famous band. I am the local news reporter. Answer my questions.

¿Cuánto tiempo hace que tu madre toca la guitarra?

¿Cuánto tiempo hace que tú cantas?

¿Cuánto tiempo hace que tu padre escribe canciones?

¿Cuánto tiempo hace que tu hermana practica baile?

¿Cuánto tiempo hace que la familia toca en un grupo de rock?

Repaso
Answer your family's questions as you prepare to go out to eat with them.

¿Todavía no estás listo(a)?

¿Te acordaste de cepillarte los dientes?

¿Pudiste ponerte los lentes de contacto?

¿Cuánto tiempo hace que te duchaste?

¿Trajiste el teléfono celular?

Holt Spanish 2 — Activities for Communication

Nombre _____ Clase _____ Fecha _____

Día a día

CAPÍTULO 5

INTERPERSONAL COMMUNICATION: ROLE-PLAYS

Vocabulario 1/Gramática 1

STUDENT A Your mother, **Student B,** is upset because you didn't get your chores done. Answer **Student B**'s questions about why you couldn't do your chores. Each time tell **Student B** that you couldn't do the chore because someone else didn't bring what you needed.

STUDENT B Your child, **Student A,** didn't get anything done this afternoon. Ask **Student A** why he or she didn't vacuum his or her room, do the dishes, feed the dog, do his or her school work, or lock the door. Listen to each of his or her reasons.

Vocabulario 2/Gramática 2

STUDENT A The new student, **Student B,** doesn't seem to like to do anything. Ask **Student B** about five different things that he or she might be interested in. Listen to each negative response. Each time tell **Student B** that you're interested in each activity, but are interested in a different activity as well.

STUDENT B You're new at school and **Student A** wants to know what you are interested in. Using a negative expression, tell **Student A** that you aren't interested in any of the activities that he or she suggests, but that you are interested in a different activity.

Repaso

STUDENT A **Student B** is trying to market a new computer game to teens. Answer **Student B**'s questions telling him or her five different things that you like to do or are interested in. Tell **Student B** how long you have been doing each thing. Tell **Student B** what your friends like.

STUDENT B You are trying to market a new computer game to teens. Ask **Student A** three questions to find out what he or she is interested in. Find out how long **Student A** has been interested in each activity. Ask two questions to find out what his or her friends like.

Holt Spanish 2

Activities for Communication

Nombre _____ Clase _____ Fecha _____

Recuerdos

CAPÍTULO 6

INTERPERSONAL COMMUNICATION: INTERVIEWS

Vocabulario 1/Gramática 1

It is the year 2070 and you are retired and living in a community for senior citizens. My Spanish class has come to visit. Answer my questions about what life was like when you were a kid.

¿Te llevabas bien con tus padres?

¿Qué te gustaba hacer los fines de semana?

¿A qué jugabas?

De pequeño, ¿te molestaba compartir los juguetes?

Cuando tenías quince años, ¿con qué soñabas?

Vocabulario 2/Gramática 2

Last week you won a trip around the world. I am the local news reporter. Answer my questions about winning the prize.

¿Cuándo supiste la noticia del viaje?

¿Cómo te sentiste cuando lo supiste?

¿Pudiste dormir esa noche?

¿Qué te dijeron los amigos cuando oyeron la noticia?

¿Pudiste creer que ganaste?

Repaso

I am conducting a consumer survey of young people's recreational habits. Respond to the questions about what you did for fun when you were younger.

¿Coleccionabas láminas de algún tipo?

¿Tú y tus amigos iban al cine?

¿Cuántos libros leíste el verano pasado?

¿Eras aventurero(a) o solitario(a)?

¿Te gustaba jugar a los videojuegos?

Holt Spanish 2 — Activities for Communication

Nombre _____ Clase _____ Fecha _____

Recuerdos

CAPÍTULO 6

INTERPERSONAL COMMUNICATION: ROLE-PLAYS

Vocabulario 1/Gramática 1

STUDENT A Your best friend, **Student B,** is on the swim team. Unfortunately, you couldn't make it to the first competition. Ask **Student B** what the team did during the competition, and how they reacted to each other when someone won. Then ask how the other team reacted at the end of the competition.

STUDENT B Your best friend, **Student A,** couldn't come to the first swim meet, but wants to know all about it. Tell **Student A** that everyone helped each other, hugged when someone won, and told jokes afterwards. Everyone, including the other team, respected each other.

Vocabulario 2/Gramática 2

STUDENT A You and **Student B** are having lunch when you read in the paper that his or her favorite singer is sick. Ask how **Student B** felt when he or she heard the news. After **Student B** responds, tell **Student B** how you felt last year when you found out your favorite football player hurt his knee.

STUDENT B You and **Student A** are having lunch when he or she discovers in the paper that your favorite singer is sick. Tell him or her that you didn't want to believe it. Ask **Student A** how he or she felt when he or she found out his or her favorite football player hurt his knee.

Repaso

STUDENT A You and **Student B** are remembering how easy grade school was. Tell **Student B** that you always made good grades. Ask **Student B** what kind of grades he or she made. Then tell **Student B** four things that you and your friends did during recess and ask **Student B** what recess was usually like at his or her school.

STUDENT B You and **Student A** are remembering how easy grade school was. Listen to **Student A**'s question. Respond by telling **Student A** that you made good grades too. Then, listen to **Student A** describe his or her recess. Describe four things that you did at recess with your friends.

Holt Spanish 2

Activities for Communication

¡Buen provecho!

CAPÍTULO 7

INTERPERSONAL COMMUNICATION: INTERVIEWS

Vocabulario 1/Gramática 1

You are helping your mom prepare a dinner party for her friends. Answer her questions using double object pronouns.

¿Me compraste el té?

¿Me trajiste las fresas del supermercado?

¿Te lavaste las manos?

¿Me lees los ingredientes de esa receta?

¿Me dejaste los platos en el comedor?

Vocabulario 2/Gramática 2

You are a famous television chef. Answer the following questions from the audience during one of your shows.

De niño, ¿comías una dieta balanceada?

¿Alguna vez serviste un plato quemado?

¿Prefieres la carne horneada o asada?

Para hacer un gazpacho, ¿es importante añadir ajo picado?

No me gustan los huevos fritos. ¿Qué otro tipo de huevos hay?

Repaso

You just ate the worst meal of your life. And it was expensive, too! Answer your friend's questions to tell him or her about this horrible meal.

¿Qué tal estaba el bistec en el Restaurante Todobueno?

¿Qué le dijiste al camarero mientras esperabas otro bistec?

¿Qué le faltaba a la sopa?

¿Había muchos clientes en el restaurante?

¿Dejaste una propina grande?

Nombre _____ Clase _____ Fecha _____

¡Buen provecho!

CAPÍTULO 7

INTERPERSONAL COMMUNICATION: ROLE-PLAYS

Vocabulario 1/Gramática 1

STUDENT A You and **Student B** are planning on having lunch together. He or she is really particular and doesn't like to try new things. Recommend four dishes to **Student B**. Describe how each dish usually tastes. After **Student B** rejects your suggestions, say that he or she always eats the same thing.

STUDENT B You and **Student A** are going to have lunch. **Student A** always wants you to try new things. Reject each of **Student A**'s suggestions with an explanation of why each food tastes bad to you.
　　　　generalmente　　　típicamente　　　constantemente

Vocabulario 2/Gramática 2

STUDENT A **Student B** is your grandma and is telling you how to make chicken noodle soup. Ask if you should cut the chicken. Listen to the answer, then ask when to add the noodles. Ask how long the soup needs to boil. Finally, tell her that it tastes weak and ask what to do.

STUDENT B **Student A** is your grandchild and needs your help with cooking chicken noodle soup. Tell him or her how to prepare the soup. Tell **Student A** that you cut the chicken, boil the water, then you add the noodles. The soup should generally boil thirty minutes. If it's weak, it needs salt.

Repaso

STUDENT A You want to surprise **Student B** with a dinner out, but don't know where to go. Ask **Student B** to tell you about the best meal he or she ever had at a restaurant. Ask **Student B** to describe the restaurant's interior. Ask what foods were served and why they were so good. Answer **Student B**'s questions.

STUDENT B **Student A** wants to know about your favorite restaurant experience. Listen to **Student A**'s questions. Tell **Student A** what the restaurant was like. Describe your meal. Then ask **Student A** to describe his or her favorite restaurant experience.

Holt Spanish 2　　　　　　　　　　　　　　　　　　　　Activities for Communication

Nombre _____ Clase _____ Fecha _____

Tiendas y puestos

CAPÍTULO 8

INTERPERSONAL COMMUNICATION: INTERVIEWS

Vocabulario 1/Gramática 1
You just got back from the mall with your friends. Answer your sibling's questions about what you did.

¿Adónde fuiste?

¿Qué buscabas?

¿Lo encontraste?

¿Fuiste a muchas tiendas?

¿Qué hacían tus amigos?

Vocabulario 2/Gramática 2
Answer the following questions from a phone survey about shopping habits.

¿Prefieres ir de compras por la mañana o por la tarde?

¿Para quién sueles comprar cosas?

¿Te gusta ir de compras por una hora, tres horas o más de cinco horas?

¿Necesitas pasar por el mercado para ir al colegio?

¿Cuánto esperas gastar en el mercado?

Repaso
You are a famous local artisan. Answer the following questions for a radio interview.

¿Qué hacías antes de hacer tus famosas figuras talladas?

Cuando ibas al mercado con las figuras, ¿la gente las compraba rápidamente?

¿Siempre pensaste que ibas a ser artista?

¿Cuánto tiempo trabajas al día?

¿Te gustan las figuras de madera o prefieres las de piedra?

Holt Spanish 2   Activities for Communication

Nombre _____ Clase _____ Fecha _____

Tiendas y puestos

CAPÍTULO 8

INTERPERSONAL COMMUNICATION: ROLE-PLAYS

Vocabulario 1/Gramática 1

STUDENT A You're on the phone with **Student B**. Today you tried to buy some new clothes at the mall but your younger sister kept interrupting and giving you her opinion. Tell **Student B** about your trip to the mall. Describe four pieces of clothing that you tried on, which ones you were going to buy, and what happened to change your mind.

STUDENT B You're on the phone with **Student A** who just went shopping. He or she is very frustrated. Ask what happened on the shopping trip. Find out what clothes he or she tried on. Ask which ones he or she bought and why or why not.

Vocabulario 2/Gramática 2

STUDENT A You're at the local flea market with **Student B** and you keep seeing things that you like. Ask **Student B** what he or she thinks of four things that are in the stand in front of you. Listen to the answers. Then state whether or not you are going to buy the one in front of you, or look at a different stand.

STUDENT B You're at the local flea market with **Student A** who sees lots of things that he or she likes. For everything that he or she asks you about, tell **Student A** that you saw similar items at a different stand that you like better. Give your opinion on which to buy.

Repaso

STUDENT A You asked your grandchild, **Student B,** to buy four items at the market for you. Ask **Student B** if he or she purchased the items. Ask **Student B** to tell you what happened while he or she was shopping to keep him or her from buying them for you.

STUDENT B You were supposed to buy some items for your grandmother, **Student A,** at the market. However, you got sidetracked with some friends, and spent some of the money on food and videogames. Finally, when you went to buy the items, the market was closed. Answer **Student A**'s questions and explain what happened.

Holt Spanish 2 Activities for Communication

A nuestro alrededor

INTERPERSONAL COMMUNICATION: INTERVIEWS

Vocabulario 1/Gramática 1
You are a radio weather reporter. Answer the following questions about the bad weather the city is having.

¿Hay más tormentas este año que el año pasado?

¿Vamos a ver menos tornados que tormentas?

¿Siempre hay tantos relámpagos como truenos?

¿Llueve más aquí que en otras ciudades?

Normalmente, ¿hay más niebla que sol en esta ciudad?

Vocabulario 2/Gramática 2
You and your family are going camping this weekend. Answer these questions from a friend who has never gone camping.

¿Dónde dormirás?

¿Qué llevarán para comer?

¿Qué harán durante el día?

¿Qué harás si hace mal tiempo?

¿Me llevarás a hacer camping algún día?

Repaso
You are a famous author. Answer the interview questions about your new suspense novel.

¿Cómo empieza la historia?

¿Qué pasa entonces?

¿Pasa algo de repente?

¿Y después?

¿Qué pasa al final?

Nombre _____ Clase _____ Fecha _____

A nuestro alrededor

CAPÍTULO 9

INTERPERSONAL COMMUNICATION: ROLE-PLAYS

Vocabulario 1/Gramática 1

STUDENT A Student B is telling you a story about a disastrous trip to the desert. Ask Student B to tell you what happened at the beginning of the trip when everything was going fine. Ask him or her to describe two things that happened in the middle of the trip to make it such a disaster. Finally, find out how the trip ended.

STUDENT B Tell Student A about your horrible trip to the desert. Say that the trip started out fine. You were hiking and rock climbing. Then tell him or her two things that went wrong in the middle of the trip to ruin everything. Conclude the story.

Vocabulario 2/Gramática 2

STUDENT A You're spending a day at the beach with Student B. Using the subjunctive, tell Student B what you hope you two are able to do. Listen to Student B's response after each suggestion and come to an agreement. Make at least five suggestions about what you hope to do.

STUDENT B You're spending the day at the beach with Student A. Listen to what Student A wants to do. Respond by saying what you prefer to do, using the subjunctive. Then come to an agreement about each suggestion.

Repaso

STUDENT A You are a travel agent booking a tropical vacation for Student B. Tell Student B what happened to your clients that went to the same beach. On the trip, three good things happened to them, and two unfortunate events. In the end, they enjoyed the trip.

STUDENT B You are booking a vacation through Student A, your travel agent. He or she is telling you what happened to the last clients that took the same trip. For every good event that happened to them, say that you hope the same thing happens to you. For every unfortunate event, say that you hope it doesn't happen to you.

Holt Spanish 2 — Activities for Communication

Nombre _____ Clase _____ Fecha _____

De vacaciones

CAPÍTULO 10

INTERPERSONAL COMMUNICATION: INTERVIEWS

Vocabulario 1/Gramática 1

To help your travel agent plan the ideal vacation for your family, answer the following questions.

¿Tu familia ha hecho planes para ir a Argentina en el verano o en el invierno?

¿Dónde han buscado información sobre Buenos Aires?

¿Tú y tus padres ya han hecho reservaciones en un hotel o en una pensión?

¿Prefieres que el avión llegue a Buenos Aires por la mañana o por la tarde?

¿Es buena idea que tú y tus padres empiecen el viaje en la costa o en la ciudad?

Vocabulario 2/Gramática 2

Imagine that you spent two weeks in Argentina last summer. A new student from Argentina wants to know about your stay. Answer the questions.

¿Por cuánto tiempo estuviste en Argentina?

¿Qué pasó el día que fuiste a las cataratas?

¿Qué tiempo hacía?

¿Fuiste de compras? ¿Cómo eran los mercados y los precios?

¿Sigues pensando en ir a Córdoba el próximo verano o prefieres volver a Argentina?

Repaso

You work in your city's tourist office. I am a Spanish-speaking tourist. Answer my questions.

¿Me recomienda usted que me hospede en una pensión o en un albergue juvenil?

¿Has ido alguna vez al Museo de Arte Moderno? Si quiero visitarlo, ¿me aconseja usted que tome un taxi o el metro?

¿Usted sugiere que yo visite los museos o haga un tour de la costa?

¿Es mejor que mis amigos y yo llevemos cheques de viajero o dinero en efectivo?

Voy a volver a esta ciudad en enero. ¿Qué tiempo estará haciendo?

Holt Spanish 2 — Activities for Communication

Nombre _____ Clase _____ Fecha _____

De vacaciones

CAPÍTULO 10

INTERPERSONAL COMMUNICATION: ROLE-PLAYS

Vocabulario 1/Gramática 1

STUDENT A Your cousin, **Student B,** is visiting from out of town. You have to finish a big project and are unable to show him or her around. Answer **Student B**'s questions about the best way to get around your town, and where to go.

STUDENT B You're visiting your cousin, **Student A,** from out of town. Unfortunately he or she has a big project to finish and can't show you around. Ask **Student A** the best way to get around town. Make sure to ask **Student A** the best place to eat lunch, at least two sites to see, and one other personal recommendation.

Vocabulario 2/Gramática 2

STUDENT A Your grandfather, **Student B,** called and you answered the phone. Now he wants to know what you are doing. Tell **Student B** that you're watching television. Using the future tense, answer **Student B**'s questions about what you plan to do this summer. Say two things that your parents recommend that you do.

STUDENT B You're on the phone with your grandchild, **Student A.** Listen to what **Student A** is doing. Tell him or her that you are having coffee. Find out at least two things he or she plans to do this summer. Ask what **Student A**'s parents want him or her to do.

Repaso

STUDENT A Ask **Student B** if he or she is still thinking about going to Argentina this summer. Find out if **Student B** has any news about the vacation plans of two other friends. Finally, tell **Student B** what you think you will probably be doing this summer.

STUDENT B Tell **Student A** you've changed your plans and are now planning to go to Texas to visit your relatives. Ask **Student A** if he or she knew that another of your friends is going to Texas. Answer his or her questions about your other friends' vacation plans. Tell **Student A** that you hope he or she has a good vacation too.

Holt Spanish 2 — Activities for Communication